TREASURING THE WORD

AN INTRODUCTION TO BIBLICAL MANUSCRIPTS
IN THE CHESTER BEATTY LIBRARY

About the author

Dr David Hutchinson Edgar is lecturer in the New Testament in the School of Hebrew, Biblical and Theological Studies at Trinity College Dublin.

TREASURING THE WORD

An Introduction to Biblical Manuscripts
in the Chester Beatty Library

David Hutchinson Edgar

TOWN
HOUSE
DUBLIN

First published in 2003 by
TownHouse, Dublin
THCH Ltd
Trinity House
Charleston Road
Ranelagh
Dublin 6
Ireland

1 2 3 4 5 6 7 8 9 10

A CIP catalogue record for this book is available from the
British Library.

ISBN: 1-86059-164-7

Cover and text design by Wendy Williams Design
Typeset by Wendy Williams Design
Printed by Nørhaven Book, Denmark

Contents

The Christian Holy Bible has probably had a greater influence on human culture than any other single book. It has been translated into more languages and more copies of it have been published than anything else. In 1456, the Bible became the first book produced using a printing press; until this time, copies of all books were made by hand. Despite this time-consuming and painstaking process, more handmade manuscripts of the Bible, or parts of the Bible, exist than of any other ancient text. Many well-known English phrases ultimately derive from the Bible: 'apple of my eye', 'my brother's keeper', 'the writing on the wall', to name just a few, while the word itself comes from the Greek *biblia*, meaning 'books'.

The Bible remains very much part of human civilisation at the beginning of the 21st century. Millions hear readings from the Bible during Christian worship on every continent each week, while many more millions possess their own copies for private reading. Even in an increasingly secular modern culture, Christian tradition, much of which derives from the Bible, retains a strong influence. Yet the Bible is a very old book; in fact, it is really more than one book, as it is made up of a collection of separate writings gathered together into one volume. These writings were composed over a period of at least eight centuries, but they have in common the link of bearing witness to a people's relationship with their God. The authoritative nature of this witness led to these texts being collected into one volume of definitive holy writings.

The Christian Old Testament

Writings have always been of central importance for Christianity. Jesus of Nazareth was a Jew (as were the earliest Christians) and their authoritative holy writings were the Jewish scriptures. These were originally composed in Hebrew, with some small sections in Aramaic, and made up what Christians later came to call the Old Testament. These writings contain a variety of different kinds of literature: legal texts, history, prophecy, proverbs and poetry.

Traditionally, the Jewish scriptures were divided into three parts: the Law, the Prophets and the Writings. The Law, or Torah, formed the first five books of the Bible, known together as the Pentateuch. Much of the content of these five books is made up of legal codes and instructions on the correct ordering of everyday life and worship. The Prophets comprised, above all, the words of great figures such as Isaiah, Jeremiah and Ezekiel, who, speaking in God's name, warned and encouraged the people to be faithful towards God. The earliest of the prophets date back to the 8th century BC and the latest were active in the 5th century BC, after the rebuilding of the temple around 516 BC. The third category of sacred texts, the Writings, was composed of a variety of types of literature. Among the best known of these writings are the Psalms, while other writings include the Proverbs (a large collection of wise sayings and traditions), and the dramatic stories of Job and Esther.

ADAM AND EVE
Albrecht Dürer
(1471–1528)
Engraving on paper
1504
CBL Wep 54

From the 6th century BC, the Jewish population began to spread and Jewish communities developed in other parts of the world. Many of these diaspora Jews were unfamiliar with the Hebrew language of their scriptures and, as a result, the Jewish scriptures were translated. Particularly important was the translation into Greek made in the city of Alexandria in Egypt, where there was a large Greek-speaking Jewish community. The Greek version of the Jewish scriptures is often referred to as the Septuagint (from the Latin for 'seventy'), because of a legend that tells how seventy (or seventy-two) scholars prepared the translation. The five books of the Law were probably the first to be translated, with the other books gradually being translated during the 3rd and 2nd centuries BC.

At the time of the emergence of Christianity, Greek was the most widespread language in the eastern Mediterranean area, although Jesus himself probably spoke Aramaic as his native language. As Christianity spread beyond Palestine into Syria, Asia Minor (modern Turkey), Europe, and Egypt, Greek became the common language of most early Christians. As a result, it was the

Septuagint that was used as the sacred text of the early Christians. In the writings of the early Christians, there are frequent references to the text of the Jewish scriptures, often including quotations from the Septuagint.

The Christian New Testament

Alongside the Jewish scriptures, the writings of early Christians took on great importance for Christian believers, with some of these writings eventually receiving the same authoritative status, and being collected together as the Christian New Testament. Just as several different types of writings make up the Jewish scriptures, so too a variety of literature was produced by the early Christians.

Leaders such as St Paul wrote letters to Christian communities, containing instructions, warnings, encouragement, explanations of issues that may have been misunderstood, and answers to queries from the community about particular issues. Later, copies of these letters were collected and circulated around other early Christian groups and became widely known.

Another important type of early Christian literature was the Gospel, which told of the events of the life of Jesus up to his death and resurrection, and recounted his sayings and teachings. It is likely that, from an early date, readings from these Christian writings, as well as from the Septuagint, were made when Christians gathered to worship.

THE APOSTLE PAUL
Albrecht Dürer (1471–1528)
Engraving on paper
c. 1514
CBL Wep 80

Paul is often regarded as the first great Christian missionary. He established Christian communities in many cities in Asia Minor (modern Turkey) and Greece. Thirteen letters bearing his name are preserved in the New Testament.

The Emergence of the Canon

Eventually, it became necessary for early Christians to clarify which writings should be considered authoritative (or canonical) holy scriptures, and which should not. Much of the impetus for this came from disputes during the 2nd century AD about what constituted authentic Christianity. Marcion, who drew up the first Christian canon (or list of sacred scriptures) excluded all of the Jewish scriptures, and counted only a small number of Christian writings as authoritative. His views were considered heretical, and the mainstream churches continued to regard the Jewish scriptures as authoritative for Christians. Gradually, they reached a consensus on which early Christian writings should also be considered canonical. The Gospels according to Matthew, Mark, Luke and John, and the Letters of St Paul, were widely accepted from a quite early date. Many of the other letters in the New Testament, and the Book of Revelation, received widespread acceptance only after some hesitation. Other texts, such as the Gospel of Peter, the Epistle of Barnabas, and the Shepherd of Hermas, were considered authoritative by some Christians for a while, but were eventually rejected.

BOOK OF GENESIS
(38: 9–15)
Greek text on papyrus
c.AD 300
CBL BP IV f.39v

The books of the Septuagint thus became established as the Christian Old Testament, while certain definitive early Christian writings formed the Christian New Testament. Perhaps partly in reaction to the takeover of the Greek version of their scriptures by Christians, Jews turned more and more to the original Hebrew text of these writings. This was especially so after the defeat of the

Jewish uprising by the Romans and the destruction of the temple in Jerusalem in AD 70, when their sacred texts, written in their own traditional language, were able to provide a focus of identity for the defeated nation. The Septuagint, however, had come to include some books which were originally written in Greek, or which had become popular in the Greek translation. These books, such as the Wisdom of Solomon, Ecclesiasticus, and the books of the Maccabees, were ultimately excluded from the Jewish canon, though they continued to be considered part of the Christian Old Testament. At the time of the Reformation in the 16th century, renewed interest in the original Hebrew texts led Protestant theologians to turn to the Hebrew text of the Old Testament. As a result, the Protestant churches adopted the Hebrew canon of the Old Testament, and rejected those books which were part of the Greek, but not the Hebrew, canon. These rejected books are generally referred to as the Apocrypha, that is, the 'hidden' writings.

Copying the Bible

All copies of the texts of the scriptures had to be produced by hand, which was, of course, a time-consuming task. It is quite likely that many small local churches possessed copies of only some of the biblical writings, and private ownership of manuscripts would have been rare. Most early Christians probably came into contact with the texts of scripture through hearing them read during worship, rather than through reading the texts themselves.

At the time of the emergence of Christianity, the most common form of book was the papyrus scroll. As a writing material, papyrus was prepared by laying strips of fibre from the inside of the thick stem of the papyrus reed across each other horizontally and vertically. When smoothed out and dried, sheets of papyrus were gummed together to make a long roll. Writing was done in columns, so that one column at a time could be read by unrolling the scroll with one hand, and rolling up what had already been read with the other hand.

Surviving early Christian writings on papyrus show a departure from this scroll form. The majority of early Christian papyri were made up of sheets of papyrus folded together to form a codex, that is, a book with pages, similar to what we think of as a book today. The codex was known prior to Christianity but was rarely used for long works of literature. It is unclear why early Christians began to use the codex form for their writings but, by doing so, Christianity made a significant contribution to the history of the book. The codex came to replace the scroll as the usual form for books, and papyrus was eventually replaced by parchment, which was made from animal hides specially prepared for writing. Particularly important was a kind of high-quality parchment prepared from the skins of calves, called vellum.

Because manuscripts were copied by hand, it was easy for errors to occur. A scribe could omit a line or a phrase if his eye returned to the wrong place in the manuscript he was copying. Similarly, the same words or phrases were sometimes copied twice. One scribe might add a note of his own in the margin or between the lines of the text; but another scribe, copying the manuscript at a later date, might include this scribal note as part of the text. At other times, scribes may have introduced deliberate emendations. For instance, a scribe who was familiar with a particular phrase through hearing it read, might substitute this phrase for a similar one in the manuscript he was copying.

Hostility towards Christianity from the rulers of the Roman Empire frequently led to persecution. One of the most severe persecutions occurred at the start of the 4th century AD, under Emperor Diocletian, who issued a series of decrees from the year 303, ordering the destruction of church buildings and the burning of copies of the scriptures. Christians were to be removed from public office, and their leaders were to be put on trial, unless they agreed to make a sacrifice to the Roman gods. Probably thousands of copies of the scriptures, written on papyrus, were destroyed at this time, while many others may have been hidden and ultimately lost. A complete reversal of policy came just ten years later, when Constantine granted toleration to Christians throughout the Empire in the year 313. Constantine's official recognition of Christianity increased the Church's resources and facilitated the production of copies of the biblical texts, including more elaborate and high-quality editions than had previously been common.

Translations of the Bible

EPISTLES OF SAINT JEROME
Biblia Latina
Nuremberg
Anton Koberger, 1479
CBL Incun 9

The language of the earliest-surviving Christian writings was Greek but, as Christianity spread throughout the Roman Empire and beyond, other languages also became important. In western Europe and north Africa, Latin became the language of the Church. In the East, large numbers of Christians used Syriac, while Coptic became the principal language of Egyptian Christianity, especially outside the city of Alexandria. Translations of the scriptures were made into all these languages and into others, such as Ethiopic and Armenian.

The identity of the earliest translators of the biblical writings is unknown. By the 4th century, however, several different Latin translations were in use, but their quality varied widely. St Augustine complained of this situation saying that: "Anyone who happened to gain possession of a Greek manuscript and who imagined that he had some facility in both Latin and Greek, however slight that might be, dared to make a translation."

In AD 382, Pope Damasus commissioned Jerome, one of the leading scholars of the time, to provide a revised Latin translation. The idea was to create an authoritative text that would replace the various different translations that had been made. Jerome finished his revision of the Gospels the next year, and then produced a revised translation of the Psalms, based on the Septuagint. Subsequently, he became dissatisfied with the idea of making translations of

**THE GOSPEL ACCORDING
TO MARK**
(St Mark 8: 11–26)
Greek text on papyrus
c.AD 250
CBL BP I (P45) f.6r

THE LETTERS OF ST PAUL
Letter to the Romans
(11: 24–32)
Letter to the Philippians
(4: 14–20)
Letter to the Colossians
(1: 1–2)
Greek text on papyrus
C.AD 200
CBL BP II (P⁴⁶)

THE BOOK OF REVELATION
(13: 16 – 14: 4)
Greek text on papyrus
c.AD 250
CBL BP III (P⁴⁷) f.7r

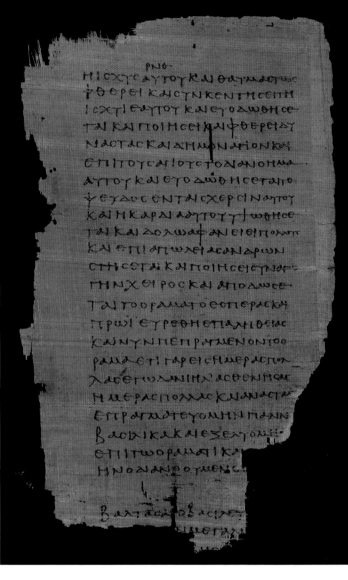

BOOK OF DANIEL
(Daniel 8: 24–5 preface)
Greek text on papyrus
c.AD 200
CBL BP X

The thirteen leaves that form part of the Book of Daniel were originally thought to be from a separate codex, but are now known to belong to the same codex as Biblical Papyrus IX. These leaves fit between the Book of Ezekiel and the Book of Esther. Further pages from this manuscript are in the University of Cologne Library.

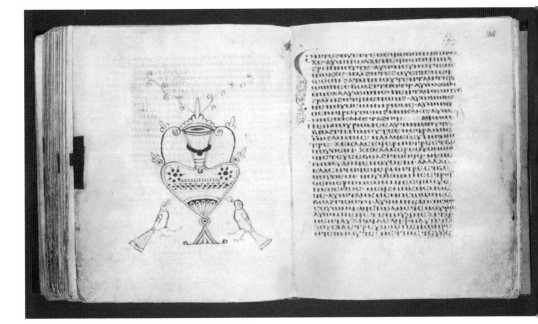

**PAULINE EPISTLES AND THE
GOSPEL OF ST JOHN**
Coptic text on parchment
c.AD 600
CBL Cpt Ms 813 ff.147v–148r

As Christianity spread, the
Bible was translated into
languages such as Coptic,
widely used in Egypt.
Gradually, decorations
began to be added to the
manuscripts, like the simple
pen ornamentation on this
page.

DECORATED STEPPED CROSS
Syriac Gospel Book
(Harklean version)
12th century
CBL Syr Ms 703

By the Middle Ages, elaborate ornamentation had become an integral part of copying biblical manuscripts, making a striking contrast with the simplicity of earlier copies of biblical texts.

de cede in sacrilegos gesta. & de prec
moysi pro poplo.   xix   :xl.

De secdo ascensu moysi in monte. &
paratione tabularu. & non adorandi
de cunctis pceptis. & de recapitulatio
instrumtorum tabernacli. & redtu mo

De collatione popli uel apparatu o
de fabricatione tabernacli qndo app
gloria domini.

EXPLICIVNT CAPITVLA
INCIPIT LIBER ELLESOO
ID EST EXODI.

EC SV
NOODI
DVODE
FILIOR
ISRAE
qui ingre
sunt in eg
cum iacob

Singli cum domibz suis introierur

CRUCIFIXION OF JESUS
Flemish Psalter
c. 1250
Gold and pigments on vellum
Latin text on parchment
CBL WMs 61 f.13v

This mediaeval artist has
united imagery from both
the Old and New Testament
as the Old Testament
prophets, identified by
their names and also the
traditional Jewish cap, point
to the new covenant in
Jesus Christ.

THE ASCENSION OF CHRIST
Master of the Duke of Bedford
Illuminated miniature from the
Coëtivy Book of Hours
Latin text
Gold, ink and tempera on vellum
c. 1443
CBL WMs 82 f.349v

Books of Hours are prayer books
for private devotions. They
contain a calendar of feast days,
Gospel lessons, psalms and
prayers.

THE SYMBOLS OF THE EVANGELISTS
School of Jean Bourdichon of Tours
From a French Book of Hours
Gold and pigments on vellum
c.1500
CBL WMs. 89 f.13

These symbols, associated with each of the four Evangelists, are based on the four living creatures that feature in the vision of the prophet Ezekiel: a man, a lion, an ox and an eagle.

ST JOHN THE EVANGELIST
Byzantine illuminated
miniature
Gold, ink and tempera on
vellum
c. 1050
CBL WMs.139 f.167v

CHRIST IN GLORY
Armenian Gospel book
c. 1615
CBL Arm 576 no. 1

ST MARK THE EVANGELIST
Armenian illuminated miniature
Gold, ink and tempera on
vellum
c. 1200
CBL Arm 558 f.265v

The artistic tradition of
depicting the Evangelists –
Matthew, Mark, Luke and
John – as scribes can be
traced back to Byzantine
models.

THE GARDEN OF EDEN
Armenian Abridged Bible
Bolorgir script on parchment
1601
CBL Arm Ms 551 f.1

ARMENIAN JEWELLED BINDING
17th century
CBL Arm 584

Leather binding with
decorated front board and
flap covered with elaborate
silver-gilt filigree work and
studded with silver bosses
and green and red stones
with a figure of the crucified
Christ in relief.

ARMENIAN GOSPEL BOOK
JEWELLED BINDING
Mid-15th century
CBL Arm Ms 567

Blind tooled-leather binding
with later additions of
bronze, silver and silver-gilt.
A large cross, applied to the
front cover, is studded with
round-headed nails and set
with five carnelians. The
corners have been
embellished with four square
silver plaques with embossed
symbols of the Evangelists.
The inscription on the cross
bears the names of the
donors.

THE RESURRECTION OF CHRIST
Albrecht Dürer (1471–1528)
From the Engraved Passion
(Illuminated)
Engraving on paper with gold
and pigments
c. 1512
CBL Wep 126

Χριστὸς καὶ Πέτρος ἐν τῇ θαλάσσῃ.
Christ and Peter upon the sea.
Christ and Peter upon the sea.

CHRISTUS UNA CUM PETRO IN MARI.
Jesus Christ et S. Pierre sur la mer.
Christus en Petrus op de Zee.

ERASMUS OF ROTTERDAM

Albrecht Dürer (1471–1528)
Engraving on paper
c.1526

CBL Wep 95

Erasmus produced one of
the first scholarly editions of
the Greek New Testament.
Luther's German New
Testament may well have
been based on Erasmus' text.

ILLUSTRATED BIBLE

Christ and Peter upon the sea
(Matthew 14, 31)
Het Nieuwe Testament ofte alle
Boecken des nieuwen verbonts
onses heeren Jesu Christi
Leyden: Elsevier, 1663

TRIPTYCH
Greek icon
mid-18th century
Tempera, gesso, gold and linen
on panel
CBL Icon 6

Small triptych that depicts the Saviour enthroned, flanked by the Virgin and St John, both full length and both in an attitude of intercession. Each wing contains a single full-length figure of a male saint inviting the viewer to contemplate the central scene.

THE DISPLAY OF EARLY
CHRISTIAN MANUSCRIPTS AT
THE CHESTER BEATTY LIBRARY,
DUBLIN

(RIGHT) **FRAGMENT OF ST
JOHN'S GOSPEL**
Greek text on papyrus
c.AD 150
CBL Ac 2555 (P66)

(FAR RIGHT) **A VIEW OF THE
PERMANENT DISPLAY OF
18TH-CENTURY GREEK AND
RUSSIAN ICONS**
CBL Icons

Old Testament books from Greek translations (rather than the original Hebrew), and prepared a new edition of the Psalms, based on the original text. The official Latin edition of the Bible prepared by Jerome became known as the Vulgate, that is, the 'common' edition. The transmission of the Latin text remained complicated, however, as scribes often incorporated passages of the Old Latin translations into Jerome's text.

GREEK GRAMMAR AND GRAECO-LATIN LEXICON ON FOUR PAULINE EPISTLES
Greek and Latin text on papyrus
c.AD 400
CBL Ac 1499

The text of the manuscript was used to help readers translate the Letters of St Paul. The Greek words or phrases are followed by the Latin translation. The appearance of tables of Greek verbs would perhaps suggest that the original reader was a Latin speaker who wanted to learn Greek.

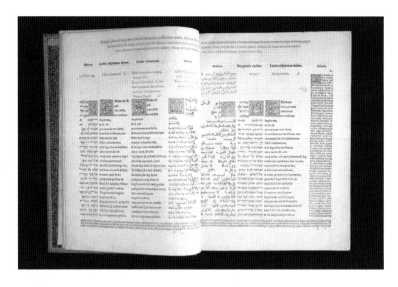

Renaissance and Reformation

The Vulgate became the main version of the Christian Bible in western
Christianity until the 16th century. The revival of interest in classical culture at
this time, known as the Renaissance, led to a renewed interest in the ancient
languages underlying the Latin text of the Bible. The invention of the printing
press around this time greatly increased the ease with which books could be
produced. An edition of the Bible in four languages (Hebrew, Aramaic, Greek
and Latin) was printed in Spain between 1514 and 1517, while, between 1516
and 1519, the noted scholar Erasmus of Rotterdam published his edition of the
Greek New Testament.

Also in the early 16th century, the theologians of the Reformation were
stressing the centrality of the Bible for Christian doctrine. In order to be as
sure as possible of the meaning of the Bible, they turned to the original
languages, rather than the Latin version. The Reformers were concerned that
the Bible should be available to all people in their own language, and thus the
translation of the scriptures was an important project for them. Martin
Luther's first German translation of the New Testament was published in 1522,
probably based on the Greek text of Erasmus, and William Tyndale's translation
of the New Testament into English was published in Germany in 1526.

The Discovery of Early Manuscripts

The early printed editions of the Greek New Testament and the early translations into modern European languages were mainly based on quite late Greek manuscripts. However, during the following centuries, a number of much earlier manuscripts came to light.

Among the most important of these is Codex Sinaiticus, dating from the 4th century and written in Greek, which was discovered by the German scholar Constantine Tischendorf in a monastery on Mount Sinai in 1844. This codex, which was presented to the Tsar of Russia but later sold by Stalin, was eventually purchased by the British Library. It contains all of the New Testament and most of the Old Testament.

Another extremely important manuscript is Codex Vaticanus, also dating from the 4th century, which comprises most of both the Old and New Testaments in Greek. This manuscript had been in the Vatican Library in Rome for several hundred years before it became well known during the 19th century. Another great vellum manuscript, Codex Alexandrinus, dating from the 5th century, had been presented by the Patriarch of Constantinople to King Charles I of England in 1627, and is also now housed in the British Library.

The Text of the New Testament

During the 19th century, examination of the early manuscripts showed that the Greek text used for early printed New Testaments and translations was inferior by comparison with these early codices, and scholars prepared new editions of the Greek New Testament. They compared the texts of the earliest manuscripts, choosing what they saw as the most reliable readings in the case of divergences between these manuscripts. The English scholars B F Westcott and F J A Hort, both professors of Divinity in Cambridge, published one of the most important editions in 1881.

The Text of the Old Testament

While manuscripts of the Greek New Testament displayed frequent variations, manuscripts of the Hebrew text of the Old Testament were much more uniform. Around the 8th century AD, Jewish scholars had issued a standardised version of the Hebrew scriptures. Until the discovery of the Dead Sea Scrolls in 1947, all the known manuscripts of the Hebrew scriptures dated from after this standardised version had been made and contained this text. Because of strict rules governing the copying of the Jewish holy scriptures, and a tradition of careful scribal practice, this text has been transmitted with considerable accuracy.

A complication arose from the fact that both the Septuagint and Vulgate translations had been made before the standardisation of the Hebrew text. Details in these translations sometimes differed from the later, standard, Hebrew text, which suggests that they might be based on an earlier version of the Hebrew scriptures. The large number of Hebrew manuscripts of the Jewish scriptures among the Dead Sea Scrolls threw further light on this issue. These scrolls, which are older than any other surviving manuscripts of the same texts, showed that the later standardised Hebrew text was basically reliable, though they also contain some variations which agree with the Septuagint, rather than the standard Hebrew text.

Papyri

At the beginning of the 20th century, only a few small pieces of papyrus containing portions of the New Testament were known from before AD 313, when official toleration had been granted to Christianity by Constantine. It was feared that substantial numbers of manuscripts of the Christian scriptures from before this period had largely perished as a result of the ten-year persecution begun by the Emperor Diocletian. By 1930, around forty fragments of papyri containing portions of New Testament texts had been discovered, but most of these were too small to be of significant use to scholars.

At this time, the earliest and most important evidence concerning the text of the Greek New Testament came from the vellum codices of the 4th century, especially Codex Sinaiticus and Codex Vaticanus. These were also the most important witnesses to the Greek text of much of the Old Testament.

The Chester Beatty Biblical Collection

Papyri

In November 1931, it was announced in *The Times* that a substantial volume of biblical papyri had been acquired by the engineer and antiquarian, Alfred Chester Beatty. Where and how the papyri were discovered is uncertain, apart from the likelihood that they came from Egypt and that they probably came from the ruins of a church or monastery. They may have made up part of a library, and were probably buried in jars for safe-keeping at some stage. The texts of the Beatty biblical papyri were published between 1933 and 1937 by Frederic Kenyon, the retired Director of the British Museum. Three papyri with portions, in Greek, of the New Testament, and eight with portions of the Old Testament, and one papyrus containing a number of non-

THE TEXT OF THE BIBLE

A NEW DISCOVERY

MORE PAPYRI FROM EGYPT

By Sir Frederic Kenyon

The last 90 years have been punctuated by discoveries of manuscripts of prime interest for Biblical students. The ball opened in 1842 with

THE TIMES
19 NOVEMBER 1931

When the purchase of the Chester Beatty papyri was made public in *The Times*, Beatty's fame as a book collector was assured.

biblical texts had been acquired by Beatty. All the papyri dated from between the 2nd and the 4th centuries AD. Such dating can be established with reasonable accuracy from the style of handwriting in the manuscripts. The New Testament papyri, dating from the 3rd century, were thus at least a hundred years older than the great vellum codices. Moreover, the Beatty papyri contained much more substantial portions of the New Testament writings than any of the previously known papyrus fragments. They thus provided a unique witness to the Greek text from the time before the mass destruction of the Christian holy scriptures during the persecution by Diocletian at the start of the 4th century.

As all the Chester Beatty papyri are in codex form, they also provided decisive evidence for the use of the codex form of book, rather than the scroll, among Christians at an early date. They do, however, show some variation in the technique used to form the pages of the codex, which probably reflects their early date, before one method of production became standard. In some cases, all the sheets of papyrus were placed in a pile and folded over in the centre, like newspapers or magazines are formed today. The papyrus containing the Gospels and Acts, however, was formed by folding single sheets in the middle, and then sewing these together at the fold. Several of the other codices were formed in the manner which

HUGO IBSCHER EXAMINING CHESTER BEATTY'S PAPYRI
c.1930

The Chester Beatty Library is committed to preserving this unique collection of world heritage items, but age and the physical damage they suffered before Beatty acquired them has weakened the structure of many pieces. The pre-eminent German conservator, Hugo Ibscher, was commissioned by Beatty to clean, repair and mount the pages in glass frames for their protection.

eventually became conventional. This involved folding four or five sheets together to make up sixteen or twenty pages. A number of such bundles of pages, called quires, were then sewn together at the fold to make up a larger book.

• THE GOSPELS One of the most striking of the Beatty papyri is the codex containing the four Gospels of Matthew, Mark, Luke and John, and the Acts of the Apostles (Chester Beatty Biblical Papyrus I, also known to scholars as P[45]). Until its discovery, only small fragments of the single Gospels on papyrus were known, and it was believed that all four Gospels had not been collected into one book until a later date. The Beatty papyrus, dating from around AD 200, showed that the four Gospels and the Acts of the Apostles had been compiled in one volume much earlier than many expected. Although many more papyrus fragments have since been discovered, this codex remains the only surviving example of the four Gospels and the Acts on papyrus in one volume. Unfortunately, only small portions of St Matthew's and St John's Gospels have survived, but the texts of St Mark and St Luke, and the Acts, are more extensive.

What is generally accepted as the oldest-surviving New Testament manuscript is a single small fragment of a page of St John's Gospel, dating from around

THE GOSPEL ACCORDING TO ST JOHN
(St John 11: 42–57)
Greek text on papyrus
c.AD 250
CBL BP I (P[45]) f.16v

AD 150, and housed at the John Rylands Library in Manchester (P[52]). By comparison with this fragment, portions of thirty pages of the text of the Gospels and the Acts are preserved in the Beatty papyrus P[45], which dates from less than one hundred years later.

In recent years, a number of sensational claims about the discovery of the earliest Gospel manuscript have been made. One such claim asserts that a piece of St Mark's Gospel, from a papyrus scroll, was discovered among the Dead Sea Scrolls, thus dating from the middle of the 1st century AD. This fragment, however, contains only twenty letters, less than half of which are clearly legible. The conclusive identification of such a tiny fragment is virtually impossible, and the suggestion that it is from St Mark's Gospel has not been accepted by the majority of scholars. In this light, the Beatty papyrus remains the oldest undisputed manuscript containing St Mark's Gospel, and its greater extent makes it far more valuable for the study of the Gospels and the Acts than many other surviving papyri, which contain much smaller portions of the text.

• THE LETTERS OF ST PAUL The second significant New Testament papyrus in the Beatty collection contains the text of the Letters of St Paul. Fifty-six pages of this codex were acquired by Chester Beatty, while thirty pages of the same book were acquired by the University of Michigan. Together, the Beatty and Michigan papyri make up an almost complete text of the Letters of St Paul, dating from around the year AD 200. Only four other known papyri contain portions of more than one of St Paul's letters, and two of these are of a much later date. The early date, and the fact that it contains almost the complete text of the Letters of St Paul, make this codex (Chester Beatty Biblical Papyrus II, or P[46]) extremely important for the study of the text of St Paul's letters.

An unusual feature of this papyrus is the fact that the Epistle to the Hebrews is placed second in the order of the texts in the manuscript, between Romans and I Corinthians. Today, the Epistle to the Hebrews is generally considered not to have been written by St Paul, and doubts as to whether he wrote it were expressed by several ancient theologians. The Beatty papyrus, however, indicates that at least in one area of Egypt at the start of the 3rd century,

Hebrews was included as a genuine letter of St Paul. Although the first and last few pages of the codex are missing, it seems likely that it did not contain the three 'pastoral' letters, I Timothy, II Timothy and Titus. The missing pages would not have provided enough room for these three texts.

• OTHER NEW TESTAMENT PAPYRI The third New Testament papyrus acquired by Beatty in the early 1930s contains chapters 9–17 of the Apocalypse, or Revelation of St John (Chester Beatty Biblical Papyrus III, or P^{47}). It is probable that the codex originally contained the whole of the Book of Revelation, but the beginning and end of the manuscript have been lost. Nevertheless, the portion of the text that remains is the largest single portion of the text of Revelation to have been preserved on papyrus. Only one other papyrus fragment of Revelation, containing just eight verses, is as old as the Beatty papyrus, which dates from around AD 250.

In the early 1950s, a small fragment of St John's Gospel was discovered among some papyri acquired by Beatty at that time. This fragment was subsequently identified as a missing part of a codex containing St John's Gospel, which was already known to scholars and dated from around AD 200. The rest of this manuscript (known as P^{66}), is in the Bodmer Library in Geneva, Switzerland.

• OLD TESTAMENT PAPYRI As well as the three very important New Testament papyri, Beatty's initial acquisition also contained several significant Greek manuscripts of the Old Testament. Because they were probably found along with the New Testament papyri, it is likely that they were transcribed and used by Christians, rather than being copies of the Jewish scriptures used by Greek-speaking Jews.

Two papyri, dating from around the late-3rd and early-4th centuries, contain, between them, most of the text of the book of Genesis (Chester Beatty Biblical Papyri IV and V). As the text of Genesis is incomplete in the two 4th-

BOOK OF EZEKIEL (LEFT)
BOOK OF ESTHER (RIGHT)
(Ezekiel 16: 57–17:1
Esther 3:13–13:3)
c.AD 200
CBL BP IX

The Books of Ezekiel,
Daniel and Esther (Biblical
Papyrus IX and X) were
originally part of one large
single-quire codex formed
of fifty-nine sheets of
papyrus, folded in the
middle so as to produce
118 leaves. The Ezekiel
leaves that survive in the
Chester Beatty Library
were torn in half by
dealers in the early part of
the 20th century and only
the upper portion of each
page survives.

century vellum codices, Sinaiticus and Vaticanus, the discovery of these two early papyrus texts was particularly important. Another papyrus codex (Chester Beatty Biblical Papyrus VI) contains the text of two more books of the Jewish Law: Numbers and Deuteronomy. From the style of handwriting, this can be dated to around AD 150, the oldest of the biblical manuscripts in the Beatty collection. Until the discovery of the Dead Sea Scrolls, this was the oldest-known manuscript of a part of the Old Testament.

Several papyri contain writings of the Old Testament prophets. One of the most significant is a manuscript of the Book of Daniel. This manuscript contains the early Septuagint Greek version of Daniel (Chester Beatty Biblical Papyrus X). This was later replaced by a more literal translation prepared by the scholar Theodotion around the end of the 2nd century AD. As virtually all surviving Greek manuscripts contain the text of Theodotion, the discovery of a very old manuscript of the earlier Septuagint translation was extremely important. This papyrus, dating from around the year AD 200, was at least seven centuries older than the only other manuscript of this version of Daniel known at the time.

This codex also contains portions of the text of the books of Ezekiel and Esther (Chester Beatty Biblical Papyrus IX). From around the same time comes a codex of the book of the prophet Isaiah (Chester Beatty Biblical Papyrus VII). An interesting feature of this manuscript is that notes have been added in the margin of the text, written in the Coptic language. Among the other Old Testament texts in the Chester Beatty Library is a small portion of the book of the prophet Jeremiah (Chester Beatty Biblical Papyrus VIII), also dating from around the year AD 200. The library also possesses two pages of the book of Ecclesiasticus (Chester Beatty Biblical Papyrus XI), written in the 4th century AD. This writing is one of those that became popular in the Septuagint, and is not included in the canonical Hebrew scriptures.

THE BOOK OF ENOCH
Greek text on papyrus
c.AD 300
CBL BP XII

Non-Biblical Manuscripts

In addition to the biblical papyri, the Chester Beatty collection contains manuscripts of a number of other ancient writings that are of considerable significance for the interpretation of the Bible and the history of Christianity.

• THE BOOK OF ENOCH Acquired at the same time as the major biblical papyri was a codex containing chapters 97–107 of the Book of Enoch in Greek (Chester Beatty Biblical Papyrus XII). The Book of Enoch is a Jewish apocalypse, that is, it is made up of a series of visions and revelations. It was composed in either Hebrew or Aramaic, but the complete text survives only in the Ethiopic translation. It appears to have been highly regarded in early Christianity, but its authority was eventually rejected and the text was lost, except in Ethiopia, where it remained popular. The figure of Enoch is mentioned several times in the New Testament, and a quotation from the Book of Enoch occurs in the Epistle of Jude, verses 14–15. Several manuscripts containing part of the Greek text of Enoch have been discovered, but the Beatty manuscript is the only known text of the final chapters of Enoch in Greek.

Like the codex containing the Letters of St Paul, part of this codex is owned by the University of Michigan. Alternate pages were acquired by each library, which suggests that either the finders or the dealers who sold the manuscript divided it in a rather crude manner. The codex also contains a previously unknown sermon on the festival of the Passover by Melito, a 2nd-century bishop of Sardis in Asia Minor (modern Turkey). This is probably the latest papyrus in the Beatty collection, dating from the 4th century AD.

• ST EPHREM'S COMMENTARY ON THE DIATESSARON Another unique manuscript in the Beatty collection is a copy of the Syriac text of a commentary by St Ephrem on the Diatessaron of Tatian. St Ephrem was a 4th-century Christian teacher from Syria, who wrote a large number of hymns, as well as several biblical commentaries. The Diatessaron (from the Greek words 'through four', that is 'through the four Gospels') was a harmony of the four canonical Gospels, which wove the four separate Gospel texts into one continuous narrative. It was composed in the 2nd century AD, probably in Syriac, by a Mesopotamian Christian called Tatian, and became popular in the churches of the East. For a time, it was probably used as the principal version of the Gospels in Syria and Mesopotamia. Certain of Tatian's views, however, such as his opposition to marriage and to the eating of meat, were considered heretical, and led to the suppression of his writings, including the Diatessaron. In readings for worship, the Diatessaron was replaced by translations of the four separate Gospels. Ultimately, its text was completely lost.

In the 19th century, Armenian translations of Ephrem's commentary on the Diatessaron were discovered, which preserved quotations of significant portions of the Diatessaron text. In the mid-1950s, a parchment manuscript, containing substantial portions of the original Syriac text of Ephrem's commentary on the Diatessaron, was acquired by Chester Beatty. Further pages of this manuscript were acquired during the 1980s. The manuscript dates from around the year AD 500, and is the only known Syriac manuscript of Ephrem's commentary on the Diatessaron. As the commentary includes quotations from the text of the Diatessaron, this manuscript provides unique evidence of the kind of Gospel text used in Syria between the 3rd and 5th centuries AD.

The Chester Beatty Biblical Collection: A Unique Witness to Early Christianity

The biblical manuscripts in the Chester Beatty Library bear a unique witness to the human story of the development of Christianity during the early centuries of its history. In the manuscripts of the New Testament and the Septuagint, we can envisage the library of an early Christian community, carefully copied over time and used for worship and study. We can observe how books were assembled, and see how the scribes employed certain writing techniques: the kind of abbreviations they used, how errors in the copied text were corrected, and so on.

The Beatty collection is also evidence of some of the key theological challenges that faced early Christianity. Alongside the earliest-surviving manuscript containing all of the four canonical Gospels, the Beatty collection houses the only text in the original language of Ephrem's commentary on Tatian's Diatessaron. Here we have some of the earliest textual evidence for two sides of a crucial debate in the earliest centuries of Christianity: should there be one definitive narrative of the life of Jesus, or should several narratives, each with a slightly different perspective, stand side

CHRIST WASHING THE FEET
OF THE APOSTLES
*The Miracles of Jesus
(Ta'amra Iyasus)*
Ge'ez (Ethiopic) text
on parchment
18th century
CBL Eth 913 f.111r

ST MARK THE EVANGELIST
Armenian illuminated
miniature
1628
CBL Arm 615 f.76v

by side as equally authoritative? Tatian and the Syrian Christians who, like Ephrem, used the Diatessaron, favoured a single narrative, while eventually the Christian Church as a whole came down in favour of using the four parallel narratives of the Gospels according to Matthew, Mark, Luke and John.

Translations of the biblical texts into languages, such as Coptic, Syriac, Latin and Armenian, show the spread of Christianity throughout the known world. The importance of the scriptures in all these different strands of Christianity illustrates both the unity and the diversity of the growing movement.

Comparison of the simplicity of the very early biblical papyri with the more elaborate format of some of the later versions of the scriptures itself reflects the development of Christianity and the transformation of its role in society.

THE VIRGIN ON THE CRESCENT WITH A DIADEM
Albrecht Dürer (1471–1528)
Engraving on paper
c. 1514
CBL Wep 78

Further Reading

Finegan, Jack, *Encountering New Testament Manuscripts* (London: SPCK, 1975).

Haines-Eitzen, Kim, *Guardians of Letters: Literacy, Power and the Transmitters of Early Christian Literature* (Oxford: Oxford University Press, 2000).

Horton, Charles (ed.), *The Word and its Beginnings: The Origins of the fourfold Gospel; Proceedings of a Conference at the Chester Beatty Library, Dublin 2–3 December 2000* (Edinburgh: T & T Clark, forthcoming).

Kenyon, Frederick W, *The Chester Beatty Biblical Papyri* (London: Emery Walker, 1931–38).

Metzger, Bruce, *The Early Versions of the New Testament* (Oxford: Clarendon Press, 1977).

Metzger, Bruce, *The Canon of the New Testament* (Oxford: Clarendon Press, 1987).

Metzger, Bruce, *The Text of the New Testament* 3rd edition (Oxford: Clarendon Press, 1992).